Simply seasonal

Editorial director: Brigitte Éveno

Art director: Guylaine & Christophe Moi

Production: Caroline Artémon

Editorial secretary: Sylvie Gauthier

Editorial assistant: Sophie Brissaud

Translation by Laura Washburn for JMS Books LLP

Design US edition Chris Bell

The editors would like to thank Maïté Lapierre
for her invaluable assistance.

© Hachette 2001
This edition © Hachette Livre (Hachette Pratique) 2003
This edition published by Hachette Illustrated UK, Octopus Publishing Group,
2–4 Heron Quays, London E14 4JP

English translation by JMS Books LLP (email: moseleystrachan@blueyonder.co.uk)
Translation © Octopus Publishing Group

A CIP catalogue for this book is available from the British Library

ISBN: 1 84430 040 4

Printed by Tien Wah, Singapore

Simply seasonal

Élisa Vergne

Photographs by Pierre Desgrieux
Styling by Valérie Lhomme

HACHETTE Illustrated

acknowledgments

Valérie Lhomme would like to thank Emmanuel Girault for his assistance, and also the following suppliers who kindly lent props: Quartz, La Forge Subtile, Monastica and Blanc d'Ivoire.

contents

summer cooking

recipe list

introduction

Summer is the season for friends, weekends, vacation time. You won't want to spend all your time cooking. Simplicity, flavor, hospitality, originality—all these qualities can be combined in a single dish, making it easy to organize effortless summer cooking, with something for everyone. First, a bit of shopping; next, a little preparation. Then everyone can help out by assembling the kebabs or preparing the grill. This sunny style of cooking is based around pâtés and terrines, and grain-based salads, making it not only perfect for summer parties but also for picnics. Cold dishes—stuffed poultry or meat and savory mousses—also play their part. Imagine a long table, colorfully decorated, on the patio or terrace, a linen cloth laid out in a clearing or on the beach. Just add bread, a vegetable salad, a bottle of chilled wine, and some fruit. You'll be free to relax, to join in the conversation, to enjoy yourself with your friends, because summer cooking is an occasion to be shared by all.

Chilled fish savarin with Mexican sauce

• Poach the salmon and white fish fillets in simmering salted water for 10 minutes. Meanwhile, trim and wash the spinach. Blanch for 1 minute in boiling water, then drain and spread out to dry on a dish towel. Grease a 7-cup ring mold with the butter and line with the spinach leaves.

Serves 6
Preparation: 20 minutes
Cooking time: 1 hour 10 minutes

10 oz salmon fillet
1 lb white fish fillets
4 oz fresh spinach
1½ tablespoons unsalted butter
7 eggs
6 sun-dried tomatoes, chopped
12 black olives
1 teaspoon ground cinnamon
2 pinches of grated nutmeg
½ teaspoon turmeric
cayenne, salt, and black pepper
10 oz button mushrooms
juice of 1 lemon
1 tablespoon olive oil

• For the Mexican sauce:
3 red bell peppers
3 lb tomatoes
2 cups minced onions
4 tablespoons olive oil
6 garlic cloves, chopped
2 tablespoons white wine vinegar
3 sprigs of fresh thyme
2 pinches of sugar
2 pinches of hot chili powder
salt and freshly ground pepper

• Preheat the oven to 350°F. Drain the fish and flake with a fork, discarding skin and bones.

• Beat the eggs. Add any remaining spinach along with the flaked fish, sun-dried tomatoes, olives, turmeric, cayenne, salt, and pepper. Pour into the mold. Cover and set in a bain marie (or a roasting pan half filled with water). Bake for 40 minutes. Remove from the oven and let cool.

• For the sauce: Broil and peel the bell peppers, then chop them. Peel and mince the tomatoes. Cook the onions in the olive oil for 3 minutes, then add the garlic and cook for 1 more minute. Add the vinegar and cook until it has evaporated. Stir in the tomatoes, thyme, sugar, chili powder, salt, and pepper. Simmer for 10 minutes. Let cool, then stir in the peppers.

• Clean the mushrooms and slice thinly. Toss with the lemon juice, oil, and salt, and let marinate for 15 minutes. Gently remove the fish savarin from the mold, fill the center with the mushrooms, and serve with the sauce.

Rice salad with poached eggs

• Cook the rice in boiling salted water until tender. Drain and rinse. Stir in 2 tablespoons of the olive oil and set aside to cool.

• Slice the tops off the tomatoes and scoop out the flesh. Season the inside of each with salt and a pinch of sugar. Mince the tomato tops.

• Cook the onion in 1 tablespoon of the olive oil until soft. Add the minced tomatoes and half the bell peppers. Season. Cook over low heat for 20 minutes. Meanwhile, cook the green beans in boiling salted water for 4 minutes. Drain and refresh under cold running water.

• Bring a large, wide pan of water to a simmer. Add the vinegar. Break the eggs, one by one, into a cup and then slide carefully into the simmering water. Poach for 3 minutes. Remove and drain on paper towels.

• Dry the insides of the tomato shells, then fill with the tomato–pepper mixture. Place a poached egg in the top of each stuffed tomato. Mix the mayonnaise with the whisky and ketchup, and place a dollop on each egg.

• Mix the rice with the remaining bell peppers, the green beans, and olives. In a small bowl, combine the curry powder, lemon juice, salt, and pepper. Gradually whisk in the remaining 3 tablespoons olive oil and the sunflower oil until thick. Pour this over the rice salad and toss to mix. Serve with the stuffed tomatoes.

Serves 4
Preparation: 20 minutes
Cooking time: 30 minutes

1$\frac{1}{3}$ cups long-grain rice
7 tablespoons olive oil
4 large tomatoes
1 onion, chopped
2 red bell peppers, diced
1 cup fine green beans, cut in $\frac{1}{2}$-inch pieces
1 tablespoon vinegar
4 eggs
3 tablespoons mayonnaise
$\frac{1}{2}$ teaspoon Scotch whisky
$\frac{1}{2}$ teaspoon ketchup
$\frac{1}{3}$ cup sliced stuffed green olives
$\frac{1}{3}$ cup sliced black olives
$\frac{1}{2}$ teaspoon curry powder
3 tablespoons lemon juice
2 tablespoons sunflower oil
sugar
salt and freshly ground pepper

Vegetable kebabs with red sauce

• Bring 3 cups of water to a boil and add the bouillon powder and salt. Rain in the polenta or cornmeal, stirring constantly, and cook for 5 minutes. Stir in 1 tablespoon of olive oil. Spread out in a pan to make a ½-inch layer and let cool.

• Cook the cauliflower florets in boiling salted water for 5 minutes; drain. In a large bowl, whisk half the garlic with 5 tablespoons of the oil, the lemon juice, and cumin. Add the cauliflower, zucchini, bell pepper squares, mushrooms, and onions. Let marinate for 1 hour.

• For the sauce, preheat the oven to 475°F. Combine the tomatoes, diced pepper, ½ teaspoon sugar, the remaining garlic, the thyme, salt, and pepper in a baking dish. Drizzle with 1 tablespoon olive oil. Bake for 5 minutes, then transfer to a bowl and stir in the vinegar and 3 more tablespoons of oil.

• Thread the marinated vegetables onto skewers. Cook under a preheated broiler for 10–12 minutes, turning often and basting with the remaining oil. Slice the set polenta and brown in the hot butter for 3 minutes. Sprinkle with the Parmesan shavings and serve with the vegetable kebabs and red sauce.

Serves 4
Preparation and cooking time: 30 minutes
Marinating time: 1 hour

2 tablespoons unsalted vegetable bouillon powder
1¼ cups polenta or yellow cornmeal
12 tablespoons olive oil
1 small cauliflower, in florets
4 garlic cloves, crushed
3 tablespoons lemon juice
2 pinches of ground cumin
2 long, thin zucchini, cut into ¾-inch rounds
2 bell peppers (1 red, 1 yellow), cut into 1¼-inch squares
8 small button mushrooms
4 small onions, halved
1 lb tomatoes, diced
1 red bell pepper, diced
2 sprigs of fresh thyme
1 tablespoon wine vinegar
1½ tablespoons unsalted butter
½ cup Parmesan shavings
sugar, salt, and freshly ground pepper

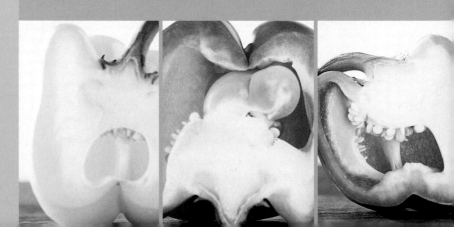

Country-style lamb terrine

Serves 6
Preparation: 20 minutes
Cooking time: 2¼ hours
Chilling time: 24 hours

3 garlic cloves, crushed

1 teaspoon coarsely crushed black pepper

2 whole cloves

2¾ lb boneless lamb shoulder, trimmed of excess fat

2 tablespoons olive oil

2 onions, sliced

4 carrots, thinly sliced

½ calf's foot, blanched

2 cinnamon sticks

1 star anise

1 fresh bouquet garni (bay leaf and 2 sprigs each of thyme and parsley)

1 bouillon cube

3 cups dry white wine

salt and freshly ground pepper

• Put the garlic, crushed pepper, and cloves in a piece of cheesecloth and tie into a bundle.

• Cut the lamb into cubes. In a pan, heat the oil, add the lamb, and brown on all sides. Add the onions and carrots, and cook, stirring constantly, until golden. Season with salt and pepper. Add the calf's foot, cheesecloth bundle, cinnamon sticks, star anise, bouquet garni, crumbled bouillon cube, and white wine. Bring slowly to a boil. Half-cover the pan and simmer gently for 2 hours.

• Using a slotted spoon, remove the cubes of lamb, the onions, and carrots from the liquid and set aside. Lift out the calf's foot, remove the meat from the bone, and mince. Arrange some of the carrots on the bottom of a terrine mold or loaf pan. Cover with half of the lamb cubes, then layer on the meat from the calf's foot mixed with the remaining carrots and the onions. Finish with the remaining lamb cubes.

• Skim off the fat from the cooking liquid. Strain the liquid, then pour into the mold. Let cool, then cover and refrigerate for 24 hours. Serve sliced, accompanied by a green salad, cucumbers, and tomatoes.

Serves 6
Preparation: 20 minutes
Cooking time: 1½ hours
Chilling time: 12 hours

2 chicken bouillon cubes • 1 fresh bouquet garni (2 bay leaves, 3 sprigs of rosemary, and 2 sprigs of thyme) • 1 small, hot, red chili pepper • 1 teaspoon green peppercorns • 1 chicken, about 3 lb • 14 oz canned foie gras • 1 teaspoon powdered gelatin • dash of Tabasco • 2 tablespoons port • 1 sprig of fresh tarragon • salt and freshly ground pepper • **For the salad:** 1 head romaine lettuce • 1 tablespoon wine vinegar • 1 tablespoon port • 1 teaspoon Dijon mustard • 1 tablespoon walnut oil • 2 tablespoons olive oil • ½ cup walnut pieces • handful of raisins

Chicken and foie gras pâté

• Bring 4 cups of water to a boil and add the bouillon cubes, bouquet garni, chili pepper, and green peppercorns. Salt lightly. Add the chicken, cover, lower the heat, and simmer for about 1¼ hours.

• Let the chicken cool in the cooking liquid, then lift it out. Reserve the liquid. Remove the skin from the chicken and carefully take the meat from the bones. Slice the meat into strips. Alternate thin layers of chicken strips with slices of foie gras in a terrine mold or loaf pan. Press down to compact, then smooth the surface.

• Skim and strain the cooking liquid, then measure 1¼ cups. Add the gelatin and

bring gently to a boil, stirring to dissolve. Add the Tabasco and port, then let cool.

• Strip the tarragon leaves from the stem and arrange in a decorative pattern on top of the pâté. Carefully pour on the cooled gelatin mixture. Cover and refrigerate for 12 hours.

• Just before serving, prepare the salad. Wash and dry the lettuce leaves, then cut or tear into pieces. Make a dressing by mixing together the vinegar, port, mustard, salt, and oils. Add the walnut pieces and raisins, and toss with the lettuce. Serve with the pâté, accompanied by slices of warm toast.

Bulgur wheat salad with chicken and almonds

- Soak the bulgur wheat according to package directions.
- Broil the bell peppers, turning frequently, until their skins are charred. Peel, seed, and mince.
- Combine the raisins with the vinegar in a bowl and set aside to steep. Peel and chop the tomatoes. Sprinkle with salt and set aside to drain.
- Combine the walnut oil and 3 tablespoons of the olive oil in a large bowl. Add the Tabasco, the raisins and vinegar, the tomatoes, bell peppers, almonds, parsley, chives, salt, and pepper. Add the bulgur wheat and toss thoroughly to blend. Cover and refrigerate for 2 hours.
- Soften the shallots in the remaining tablespoon of olive oil. Add the chicken breasts and cook over low heat for 10 minutes, turning once halfway through cooking. Season with salt and let cool.
- Just before serving, cut the chicken into thin slices on the diagonal and toss into the bulgur salad. Garnish with a few parsley leaves.

Serves 4
Preparation: 30 minutes
Cooking time: 30 minutes
Chilling time: 2 hours

2 cups fine bulgur wheat
2 red bell peppers
3 tablespoons raisins
3 tablespoons wine vinegar
4 tomatoes
1 tablespoon walnut oil
4 tablespoons olive oil
dash of Tabasco
$\frac{1}{2}$ cup slivered almonds
2 tablespoons minced fresh parsley, plus a few leaves for garnish
1 tablespoon minced fresh chives
2 shallots, minced
4 boneless chicken breast halves
salt and freshly ground pepper

Ham and mortadella pâté with herbs

• Thaw the spinach. Place in a pan and cook according to package directions; drain. Mince the herbs and add to the spinach along with the nutmeg, cinnamon, sugar, salt, and pepper.

• Preheat the oven to 350°F. Grease a 4-cup capacity loaf pan with the butter. Sprinkle cracker crumbs over the bottom and sides of the pan to coat evenly.

• Mince the ham and mortadella in a food processor. Add to the spinach mixture, along with the beaten eggs and the pine nuts. Pour into the pan and set in a bain-marie (or a roasting pan half filled with water). Bake for 45 minutes. Let cool, then cover and refrigerate.

• For the sauce, combine the mustard and oil. Add the yogurt and herbs.

• Line a serving platter with lettuce leaves. Unmold the pâté onto the platter. Sprinkle with the toasted pine nuts and surround with the tomato and egg slices. Serve the sauce separately.

Serves 6
Preparation: 45 minutes
Cooking time: 1 hour

1 lb frozen leaf spinach
1 sprig each of fresh dill and tarragon
2 sprigs of fresh flat-leaf parsley
pinch of grated nutmeg
3 pinches of ground cinnamon
$^{1}/_{2}$ teaspoon sugar
$1^{1}/_{2}$ tablespoons unsalted butter
unsweetened cracker crumbs
7 oz cooked ham
4 oz mortadella
5 eggs
$^{1}/_{3}$ cup pine nuts
salt and freshly ground pepper

• For the sauce
1 tablespoon Dijon mustard
5 tablespoons olive oil
$1^{1}/_{2}$ cups plain yogurt
1 teaspoon each chopped fresh tarragon, dill, and parsley

• For the garnish
lettuce leaves
1 tablespoon pine nuts, toasted
6 ripe tomatoes, sliced
3 hard-cooked eggs, sliced

Helpful hints
for summer

• Warm weather is ideal for feasting with friends in a cool garden room or outdoors on the patio or deck, in the shade of some trees.

• Summer dishes can easily be made in advance, and it is usually best to do preparations in the cool of the evening or first thing in the morning, before the sun reaches its full intensity. This is the best time to make dishes that are to be served cold, so they have plenty of time to chill. In fact, many cold dishes, especially pâtés and cold meats, improve with a bit of time, as this allows flavors to mingle and mature. When chilling dishes in advance, be sure to cover them tightly, with foil or plastic wrap, which will keep moisture in and prevent odors from escaping. Remember to remove the dishes from the refrigerator about 30 minutes in advance of serving: most flavors are at their best when not over-chilled. Sauces, vegetables, and garnishes are best prepared just before serving. Any recipe that calls for broiling can just as easily be cooked outdoors on the grill.

• For pâtés set with gelatin, dip the mold in hot water for 10 seconds—no longer—to make it easier to unmold. For all other pâtés and terrines, run the blade of a knife around the sides, between pâté and mold, to loosen.

• After dipping the mold in hot water, or loosening with a knife, place the upturned serving plate on top of the mold. Holding the mold and plate securely together, turn them over and shake gently. You'll hear a small "plop" when the pâté lands on the plate.

Greek-style lamb kebabs with tzatziki

• The day before serving, put the lamb in a bowl and add the garlic, coarse salt, vinegar, wine, 1 tablespoon olive oil, the sugar, coarse pepper, chopped bay leaf, thyme leaves, and chili pepper. Mix well, then cover with plastic wrap and marinate in the refrigerator overnight.

Serves 4
Preparation: 15 minutes
Marinating time: 12 hours
Cooking time: 12–15 minutes

1¹/₂ lb boneless leg of lamb, cubed
4 garlic cloves, crushed
1 tablespoon coarse salt
1 tablespoon vinegar
1 cup dry white wine
3 tablespoons olive oil
¹/₂ teaspoon sugar
¹/₂ teaspoon coarsely ground black pepper
1 bay leaf
1 sprig of fresh thyme
1 hot, red chili pepper
1 red bell pepper, cut into 1-inch squares
1 green bell pepper, cut into 1-inch squares
1 yellow bell pepper, cut into 1-inch squares
4 pita breads
8 lettuce leaves, shredded

• **For the tzatziki**
1 small hothouse cucumber
¹/₂ teaspoon sugar
1 teaspoon garlic powder
1 cup plain yogurt
2 tablespoons olive oil
salt

• The following day, drain the meat and thread onto skewers with the squares of bell pepper, alternating the colors.

• For the tzatziki: Peel and grate the cucumber, and toss with the sugar, garlic, and salt. Put in a strainer and set aside to drain.

• Heat the grill (or broiler). Brush the kebabs with oil and grill for 12–15 minutes, turning often and basting with oil regularly.

• Finish the tzatziki: Combine the yogurt with the olive oil and stir in the cucumber mixture. Warm the pita breads, split open, and fill each with 2 of the kebabs and shredded lettuce (or green salad of your choice). Serve immediately, with the tzatziki and a salad of tomatoes, onions, and feta cheese.

Fish and fennel mousse
with almond sauce

• Poach the fish in a pan of simmering salted water for 7 minutes (do not boil). Let cool, then flake into largish pieces, discarding any skin.

• Trim the fennel, reserving the feathery fronds for the garnish, and cut the bulbs into quarters. Cook in boiling salted water for 30 minutes. Drain. Put the vinegar and 1 tablespoon cold water in a small bowl, sprinkle on the gelatin, and set aside to soften. Put the fennel in a food processor while still warm and reduce to a purée. Stir in the gelatin mixture, and add the turmeric and mayonnaise.

• Line a loaf pan with plastic wrap. Spoon in a layer of one-third of the fennel purée and add a layer of half the fish. Repeat the layers, then finish with the remaining fennel purée. Cover and refrigerate for 12 hours.

• Just before serving, prepare the sauce. Drizzle the vinegar and 1 tablespoon water over the bread to moisten, then squeeze out excess. Combine the garlic and almonds in a bowl. Add the bread and mix, then drizzle in the oil, stirring constantly. Season with salt.

• Unmold the fish mousse. Decorate with the reserved fennel fronds and serve in slices, with the sauce on the side.

Serves 4
Preparation: 25 minutes
Cooking time: 30 minutes
Chilling time: 12 hours

**1 lb red porgy or scup fillets
  (or use other white fish fillets)**
1½ lb fennel
1 tablespoon white wine vinegar
4 teaspoons powdered gelatin
1 teaspoon turmeric
4 tablespoons mayonnaise
salt

• For the almond sauce
3 tablespoons vinegar
3 slices of white bread
3 garlic cloves, crushed
½ cup ground almonds
7 tablespoons olive oil

Serves 6
Preparation: 30 minutes
Cooking time: 2 hours

3 red bell peppers • 4 oz thick bacon slices (about 4) • 3 tablespoons olive oil • 3 eggs, beaten • 1 boned veal shoulder roast, about 2³/₄ lb • 1 teaspoon garlic powder • 1 onion, chopped • 2 tablespoons chopped fresh flat-leaf parsley • 1 cup Banyuls or other strong, sweet red wine • salt

Spanish-style stuffed veal

• Broil the bell peppers, turning regularly until charred. Peel, seed, and cut into thin slices. Cut the bacon into fine sticks.

• Cook the bacon and bell peppers in 1 tablespoon of the oil for a minute or so, then pour in the eggs and cook until set, like a flat omelette. Let cool.

• Make a horizontal slit in the middle of the veal roast; do not cut all the way through. Open out like a book and lay flat. Sprinkle with the garlic powder and salt. Slice the omelette into strips and arrange on top of the meat. Roll up the meat to enclose the omelette (like a jelly roll). Tie into shape with kitchen string.

• Heat the remaining oil in a heavy, shallow pan and brown the veal roll on all sides. Add the onion and cook until soft, then stir in the parsley. Add the wine, cover, and simmer gently for 1¹/₂ hours. Let cool. Serve at cool room temperature, cut into slices and drizzled with the cooking juices. Accompany with a green salad.

Poached chicken breasts with tuna sauce

Serves 4
Preparation: 20 minutes
Cooking time: 30 minutes
Chilling time: 1 hour

1 lemon • 4 boneless chicken breast halves • 1 onion, chopped • 1 bay leaf • 1 cup dry white wine • $^2/_3$ cup canned tuna in water • 8 anchovy fillets in oil • $^1/_2$ cup ricotta cheese • $^1/_2$ teaspoon mustard • 1 tablespoon brandy • 3 tablespoons mayonnaise • 8 oz snow peas • 1 cup cherry tomatoes • 1 tablespoon capers • salt

• Grate the zest from the lemon. Put the chicken breasts in a pan and add the onion, lemon zest, bay leaf, white wine, and salt. Bring slowly to a boil, then simmer for 15 minutes.

• Drain the tuna and flake with a fork. Chop 4 of the anchovy fillets and put in a food processor with the tuna, ricotta, 1 teaspoon lemon juice, the mustard, and brandy. Process until smooth, then stir in the mayonnaise.

• Remove the chicken breasts from the cooking liquid and set aside to cool. Strain the liquid.

• Thin the tuna sauce by stirring in 3–4 tablespoons of the chicken cooking liquid.

• Cook the snow peas in boiling salted water for 5 minutes. Drain and refresh. To serve, pour the tuna sauce over the chicken breasts, and garnish with the remaining anchovy fillets, the cherry tomatoes, capers, and snow peas.

Serves 4
Preparation: 15 minutes
Cooking time: 3 hours

1 boneless piece of fresh ham, about 2³/₄ lb • 1 head of garlic, unpeeled, cut horizontally in half • 1 onion, studded with 4 whole cloves • 2 sprigs of fresh thyme • 2 bay leaves • 2 star anise • ¹/₂ teaspoon cumin seeds • 1 cinnamon stick • 4 black peppercorns • 4 cups hard cider • salt • 6 fresh figs • **For the rice:** 1¹/₃ cups basmati rice • 3 tablespoons olive oil • 2 teaspoons sherry vinegar • 2 teaspoons Dijon mustard • 2 pinches of curry powder • 2 tablespoons chopped fresh chives

Spiced pork with rice and figs

• Put the pork in a large, heavy pan and add the garlic, onion, herbs, spices, and salt. Pour in enough cider almost to cover the pork. Cover and bring to a boil over low heat. Simmer gently until the meat is tender, 2¹/₂–3 hours. Let cool.

• Cook the rice in boiling salted water for 10–12 minutes or until tender. Drain and rinse. In a small bowl, mix together the oil, vinegar, mustard, curry powder, and chives. Pour this mixture over the rice and toss well.

• Wipe the figs clean and trim the stems. Cut into quarters, then halve each quarter. Cut the pork into slices.

• To serve, arrange the rice in a pyramid in the middle of a serving platter and surround with the figs and pork slices.

Veal stuffed with spinach and ham

• For the stuffing, trim and wash the spinach. Cook over high heat, stirring, until wilted, then cool and squeeze dry. Cook the shallots in the butter until soft. Moisten the bread with the crème fraîche. Mix together the spinach, shallots, bread, parsley, garlic, and egg yolk, and season with salt and pepper.

• Lay the meat flat and cover with the ham. Spread with the spinach mixture. Roll up like a jelly roll and tie into shape with kitchen string.

• Brown the veal roll in the oil over medium heat. Add the onion and carrot slices, and cook for 5 more minutes. Add the stock, Madeira, garlic, bouquet garni, salt, and pepper. Cover and cook over low heat for 1$\frac{1}{2}$–2 hours. Drain the meat, reserving the cooking liquid. Let cool, then refrigerate for 12 hours.

• On the day of serving, skim the fat from the veal cooking liquid and strain, then bring to a boil. Add the carrot sticks and cook for 20 minutes. Drain and let cool. Serve the veal in slices, with the carrot sticks and olives.

Serves 6
Preparation: 45 minutes
Cooking time: 2 hours
Chilling time: 12 hours

1 boneless veal breast, about 2$\frac{3}{4}$ lb, pounded flat to form a rectangle
4 slices of cured ham
2 tablespoons sunflower oil
2 onions, sliced
8 carrots (2 sliced, 6 cut into sticks)
8 cups chicken stock
4 tablespoons Madeira
1 whole head of garlic, unpeeled, cut horizontally in half
1 bouquet garni
$\frac{1}{2}$ cup black olives
salt and freshly ground pepper

• **For the stuffing:**
1 lb fresh spinach
2 shallots, chopped
2 teaspoons unsalted butter
2 slices of white bread
1 tablespoon crème fraîche
1 bunch of fresh flat-leaf parsley, chopped
2 garlic cloves, minced
1 egg yolk

Seafood kebabs with mango sauce

• Remove any skin from the fish, then cut into 1-inch cubes. Rinse the shrimp. Put the fish and shrimp in a bowl and add the onions, oil, and salt. Mix well, then marinate in the refrigerator for 2 hours.

• For the sauce, peel the mangoes and cut the flesh from the central seed. Place in a food processor and reduce to a purée. Heat the oil in a pan, add the shallots and garlic, and cook until soft. Stir in the mango purée, cayenne, and salt. Simmer gently for 15 minutes. Let cool, then stir in the lime juice.

• Cook both the basmati rice and the wild rice in boiling salted water according to package directions. Drain and stir in the butter, raisins, and pine nuts. Keep warm.

• Heat the grill (or broiler). Drain the seafood and thread onto skewers, placing a shrimp at each end. Grill for 10–12 minutes, turning frequently.

• Serve the kebabs on the rice, accompanied by the sauce.

Serves 4
Preparation: 15 minutes
Cooking time: 20 minutes
Marinating time: 2 hours

$1\frac{1}{2}$ lb swordfish or tuna steaks, about 1 inch thick
8 large, raw shrimp in shell
2 mild onions, thinly sliced
2 tablespoons olive oil
$\frac{3}{4}$ cup basmati rice
$\frac{2}{3}$ cup wild rice
$1\frac{1}{2}$ tablespoons unsalted butter
handful of raisins
2 tablespoons pine nuts
salt

• **For the mango sauce:**
2 mangoes
1 tablespoon olive oil
2 large shallots, minced
2 garlic cloves, minced
2 pinches of cayenne
2 tablespoons lime juice

Spanish-style sole fillets

• Preheat the oven to 425°F.

• Chop the ham, olives, and capers. Mix with 1 tablespoon of the oil. Spread this mixture over the fish fillets. Roll up and secure each with a wooden toothpick.

• Place the rolls in an oiled baking dish. Pour the Madeira over, cover with foil, and bake for 7 minutes. Let cool to room temperature.

• Clean the mushrooms and slice thinly. Mix with half of the lemon juice, then add the rest of the oil, the chives, chervil, and salt, and mix well. Halve the avocados, peel, and slice thinly. Toss in the remaining lemon juice and season with salt.

• Remove the toothpicks from the fish rolls. Serve with the cooking liquid spooned over and surrounded with the avocado slices and mushrooms. Accompany with the lemon quarters.

Serves 4
Preparation: 20 minutes
Cooking time: 7 minutes

4 thin slices of cured ham

20 pimiento-stuffed green olives

1 tablespoon capers

3 tablespoons olive oil

2 whole sole or flounder, about 1 lb each, filleted and skinned

$1/2$ cup Madeira

8 oz button mushrooms

2 lemons (1 juiced, 1 quartered)

1 tablespoon chopped fresh chives

1 tablespoon chopped fresh chervil

2 avocados

salt

Italian-style prosciutto rolls

Serves 4
Preparation:
15 minutes

²/₃ cup black olives
1 cup ricotta cheese
4 teaspoons pesto sauce
2 tablespoons olive oil
12 slices of prosciutto
1 ripe cantaloupe melon
4 ciabatta or other Italian-style
bread rolls, warmed
salt and freshly ground pepper

• Preheat the oven to 400°F.

• Mince 12 of the olives; halve the remainder. Beat the ricotta to lighten it, then mix in the minced olives and pesto. Gradually beat in the oil, a spoonful at a time. Season with salt and pepper.

• Spread out the prosciutto slices. Put a small spoonful of the olive-ricotta mixture at one end of each slice and roll up neatly.

• Cut the melon in half and remove the central seeds. Slice the melon thinly. Remove the skin, if desired.

• To serve, arrange the prosciutto rolls and melon slices on plates and sprinkle with the remaining olives. Serve with the warm ciabatta.

Serves 6
Preparation: 40 minutes
Cooking time: 1½ hours

1 tablespoon unsalted butter • 2–3 tablespoons dry bread crumbs • 4 thin slices of white bread • ½ cup milk • 5 tablespoons pine nuts • 1 large onion, minced • ½ tablespoon olive oil • 2 garlic cloves, minced • 1 teaspoon sugar • 1 lb cooked ham • 1 lb ground beef • 1 teaspoon ground cinnamon • ½ teaspoon ground cumin • pinch of cayenne • 3 eggs • salt and freshly ground pepper • **For the vegetables:** 2 large eggplants • 3–4 tablespoons olive oil • 3 red bell peppers • 1¼ teaspoons sugar • 3 pinches of garlic powder • 1 tablespoon balsamic vinegar • 6 firm tomatoes • 6 tablespoons mayonnaise • 4 teaspoons mango chutney

Cinnamon-spiced meatloaf with vegetables

• Preheat the oven to 350°F.

• Grease a 5-cup capacity loaf pan with the butter and sprinkle the bottom with the bread crumbs. Soak the bread slices in the milk. Toast the pine nuts in a dry pan until golden brown.

• Soften the onion in the oil, then add the garlic and sugar, and cook until caramelized. Remove from the heat.

• Chop the ham. Squeeze the bread dry and mix with the ham, beef, onion, pine nuts, cinnamon, cumin, cayenne, salt, and pepper. Stir in the beaten eggs. Pour into the prepared pan and bake for 1 hour.

• For the vegetables, cut the eggplants into ½-inch slices. Sprinkle with salt and let drain for 20 minutes.

• Raise the oven temperature to 475°F. Rinse the eggplant slices, brush them with oil, and bake for 14 minutes, turning halfway through the cooking time.

• Char the peppers under the broiler, then peel and cut into thin strips. Sprinkle with ¼ teaspoon sugar, the garlic powder, and vinegar.

• Peel and seed the tomatoes, and cut into fine dice. Toss in a strainer with 1 teaspoon sugar and a pinch of salt, then let drain for 30 minutes.

• Mix the mayonnaise with the chutney. Drizzle 1 tablespoon olive oil over the tomatoes. Serve the meatloaf surrounded by the eggplants, peppers, and tomatoes, with the chutney mayonnaise in a bowl.

Vegetable tourte

• Preheat the oven to 400°F.

• Cook the cracked or bulgur wheat in boiling salted water according to package directions. About 5 minutes before the end of the cooking time, add the frozen vegetables. Drain and let cool.

Serves 6
Preparation: 30 minutes
Cooking time: 1 hour
10 minutes

¹/₃ cup cracked wheat or bulgur wheat
1 lb frozen, sliced mixed vegetables
6 oz tomme or other semi-soft cheese
1 avocado
1 tablespoon lemon juice
5 eggs
2 pinches of grated nutmeg
¹/₂ cup crème fraîche
¹/₄ cup evaporated milk
³/₄ cup thinly sliced black olives
3 sprigs of fresh dill
14 oz puff pastry
salt and freshly ground pepper

• **For the sauce:**
1¹/₂ cups plain yogurt
¹/₂ teaspoon garlic powder
3 tablespoons olive oil
3 sprigs of fresh dill, minced

• Finely shred enough of the cheese to measure 1 cup. Cut the rest into fine dice. Peel the avocado, cut into thin slices, and toss with the lemon juice. Beat 4 of the eggs with the nutmeg, salt, and pepper. Add the crème fraîche and evaporated milk. Fold the olives, dill, avocado, and shredded cheese into the wheat and vegetable mixture, then add the egg mixture and combine gently.

• Roll out half the puff pastry and use to line an 8-inch springform pan. Sprinkle the diced cheese over the bottom, then pour in the vegetable mixture. Roll out the remaining pastry and place on top of the pan, moistening and sealing the edges. Make a criss-cross pattern on top with the point of a knife, and brush with the remaining egg, beaten. Bake for 45 minutes. Let cool for 15 minutes before unmolding, then cool completely.

• For the sauce, combine the yogurt, garlic powder, oil, salt, and dill. Let stand for around 10 minutes. Serve the tourte with the sauce.

Ham mousse and vegetable terrine

• Cook the green beans (8 minutes), zucchini (15 minutes), and carrots (20 minutes) in boiling salted water. Drain and pat dry. Cut the zucchini and carrots into long, $\frac{1}{4}$-inch-thick slices. Dry the sun-dried tomatoes and mince.

• In a food processor, mince the ham, then add the egg whites, vinegar, oil, salt, and pepper. Gradually add the crème fraîche, mixing until smooth.

• Line a loaf pan with plastic wrap. Pour in a thin layer of the ham mousse and spread evenly. Top with a layer of green beans and then more ham mousse. Continue alternating layers of each vegetable with the ham mousse. Fold the plastic wrap over the top and refrigerate for 12 hours.

• The following day, prepare the sauce: Cook the bell peppers and onions in 1 tablespoon of oil until soft. Add the thyme and season with salt, then cover and simmer for 15 minutes. Lightly salt and sugar the cucumber and tomatoes, and set aside to drain.

• Add the vinegar and a pinch of sugar to the pepper mixture. Cook until the liquid evaporates, then purée with the cucumber and tomatoes in a food mill. Add the remaining oil. Serve the terrine with the sauce on the side.

Serves 6
Preparation: 30 minutes
Cooking time: 45 minutes
Chilling time: 12 hours

7 oz fine green beans
1 long zucchini
10 oz carrots
5–6 sun-dried tomatoes in oil
1 lb cooked ham
2 egg whites
6 tablespoons white wine vinegar
2 tablespoons olive oil
1 cup crème fraîche
salt and freshly ground pepper

• For the sauce:
2 red bell peppers, chopped
2 onions, chopped
3 tablespoons olive oil
2 sprigs of fresh thyme
1 teaspoon sugar
1 cup diced hothouse cucumber
1½ cups chopped tomatoes
2 tablespoons balsamic vinegar

Cold poached hake with cucumbers and shrimp

• Make up 8 cups of court bouillon or fish stock in a large pan. Add the hake and bring gently to a boil. As soon as the bouillon boils, remove from the heat and let the fish cool in the liquid.

• Cut the tomatoes in half; scoop out and discard the seeds. Season the tomato shells with salt and a pinch of sugar. Cook the green beans in boiling salted water for 8 minutes, then drain and refresh under cold running water. Cook the frozen vegetables in boiling water according to package directions, then drain thoroughly.

• Combine 1 tablespoon of the mayonnaise with $^1/_2$ tablespoon yogurt and the chopped dill. Add the chopped shrimp, olives, and mixed vegetables. Drain the tomato shells and fill with the shrimp mixture.

• Combine the remaining mayonnaise and yogurt. Stir in the Tabasco and brandy. Drain the hake and cut across into portions. Remove the skin. Serve on lettuce leaves, surrounded with the cucumber slices and sprinkled with chives. Garnish with the green beans, jumbo shrimp, and stuffed tomatoes, and serve with the brandy mayonnaise.

Serves 4
Preparation: 20 minutes
Cooking time: 20 minutes

court bouillon powder or fish
bouillon cube
1 hake or whiting, about 3 lb
4 large tomatoes
5 oz very fine green beans
1 lb frozen, thinly sliced
mixed vegetables
1 cup mayonnaise
1 cup plain yogurt
1 teaspoon chopped fresh dill
1 cup chopped cooked shrimp
8 cooked jumbo shrimp
8 small black olives, pitted
dash of Tabasco
1 tablespoon brandy
a few lettuce leaves
1 hothouse cucumber, thinly
sliced
snipped fresh chives
sugar, salt

winter cooking

Recipe list

introduction

Winter is the time for long, slow cooking—meat braised in its own juices, gently simmering stews, slow-baked pasta. Winter dishes are warming and sustaining. Imagine the wonderful aromas of a big pot of spicy goulash or a dish of steaming couscous topped with juicy, tender lamb, whetting the appetites of the family waiting expectantly at the table. Cooking like this is practical and convivial, allowing the cook to spend time with friends, instead of in the kitchen. We're not talking about the old-fashioned stockpot that bubbled permanently on the range and to which ingredients were added daily. Today's cold-weather dishes have a fresh, new look, drawn from all the cuisines of the world. Gratins, curries, and goulash, ragouts and tajines, phyllo pies and lasagnes, and stuffed meat—here are myriad solutions for feeding the family and for entertaining friends. After all, what could be more comforting when it's cold outside than to hear someone say: "Come for supper tonight. I've made a delicious curry."

Fish stew with garlic mayonnaise

• Rinse the porgy and sea bass, and cut into pieces. Sprinkle the fish pieces and salmon with salt, and set aside. In a large pan, combine the fish heads, wine, 4 cups of water, the onion, bay leaf, and orange peel. Bring to a boil, then simmer for 30 minutes. Strain the liquid, then return to a clean pan and add the leeks, carrots, potatoes, and salt. Cook for 25 minutes.

• For the garlic mayonnaise, crush the garlic with the cayenne and salt in a medium bowl. Slowly add the oil, drop by drop, whisking constantly. Gradually blend in the vinegar. Set aside.

• Remove the vegetables from the liquid and keep warm. Add the fish pieces and simmer gently until cooked through, 7–10 minutes depending on the thickness of the pieces.

• Gently whisk a small ladleful of the cooking liquid into the garlic mayonnaise. Return the vegetables to the stew and serve hot, accompanied by the mayonnaise.

Serves 4
Preparation: 30 minutes
Cooking time: 1 hour

1 whole red porgy or scup (or use other white fish), about 2 lb, cleaned and scaled

1 whole sea bass, about 2 lb, cleaned and scaled

2 skinless pieces of salmon fillet, about 7 oz each

1 cup dry white wine

1 large onion, studded with 2 whole cloves

1 bay leaf

1 piece of orange peel

4 leeks, white part only, sliced

4 carrots, peeled and cut up if large

4 potatoes, peeled and cut up if large

salt

• **For the garlic mayonnaise:**

4 large garlic cloves

pinch of cayenne

5 tablespoons olive oil

5 tablespoons sunflower or peanut oil

3 tablespoons white wine vinegar

Vegetable couscous with quail-egg kebabs

Serves 6
Preparation: 20 minutes
Cooking time: 1 hour

2 onions, sliced
2 bell peppers (1 red, 1 green),
coarsely chopped
2 garlic cloves, crushed
5 tablespoons olive oil
1 eggplant, cut into 1-inch cubes
$\frac{1}{2}$ celeriac, cut into 1-inch cubes
4 carrots, cut into 1-inch slices
3 zucchini, cut into 1-inch slices
$\frac{1}{4}$ cup tomato paste
2 tablespoons ras-el-hanout
spice mixture (see box opposite)
1 teaspoon ground cumin
2 pinches of cayenne
1 bouquet garni
$1\frac{1}{4}$ cups canned chickpeas
$\frac{1}{3}$ cup blanched almonds
2 cups quick-cook couscous
2 tablespoons unsalted butter
salt

• For the kebabs:
12 cherry tomatoes
6 quail eggs, hard-cooked and
peeled
4 oz firm goat cheese, cubed
12 pimiento-stuffed green olives
12 black olives, pitted

• Cook the onions, bell peppers, and garlic in 3 tablespoons of the oil for 10 minutes. Add the eggplant, celeriac, carrots, zucchini, tomato paste, ras-el-hanout, cumin, salt, and cayenne. Stir well. Add 2 cups of water and the bouquet garni, then cook, covered, for 1 hour. Add the drained chickpeas 10 minutes before the end of the cooking time.

• Toast the almonds in a dry pan.

• For the kebabs, thread the tomatoes, eggs, cheese, and olives onto wooden skewers, alternating colors.

• Heat the remaining oil in another pan, add the couscous, and cook, stirring, for 2 minutes. Add water and salt, cooking according to package directions. Fluff the grains with a fork to separate them. Add the butter, in small pieces, and the almonds, and stir.

• Serve the couscous with the vegetables and kebabs, with the cooking broth alongside.

Ras-el-hanout

1 tablespoon each ground coriander, ground cumin, ground ginger, and ground pepper • $\frac{1}{2}$ teaspoon each ground mace, grated nutmeg, ground allspice, ground cardamom, turmeric, and ground cinnamon • $\frac{1}{4}$ teaspoon each ground cloves and cayenne

• Combine all the spices (preferably freshly ground) and store in a container with a tight-fitting lid.

Spanakopita

• Thaw the spinach in a pan over low heat; drain and let cool. In another pan, soften the onions in the olive oil over low heat. Combine the dill, parsley, and green onions in a small food processor and process to obtain a coarse purée.

• Beat the eggs with a fork. Crumble in the feta. Add the herb mixture and the onions, and mix well. Season with salt and pepper. Squeeze the spinach leaves to extract as much moisture as possible, then chop coarsely. Add to the egg mixture along with the cinnamon, nutmeg, and salt, and mix well.

Serves 6
Preparation: 1 hour
Cooking time: 1 hour

1½ lb frozen leaf spinach
2 onions, minced
2 tablespoons olive oil
1 bunch of fresh dill, snipped with scissors
1 bunch of fresh flat-leaf parsley, snipped with scissors
4 green onions, coarsely chopped
3 eggs
5 oz feta cheese
2 pinches of ground cinnamon
2 pinches of grated nutmeg
10 tablespoons unsalted butter
10 sheets of phyllo pastry
salt and freshly ground pepper

• Preheat the oven to 400°F.

• Melt the butter, then strain it through cheesecoth to clarify. Butter a rectangular baking dish, about 13 x 8 inches. Trim the phyllo sheets to fit the dish. Put 5 sheets of filo pastry in the dish, buttering each one well before topping with another. Add the spinach mixture and spread out evenly. Cover with the remaining phyllo sheets, buttering well between each one.

• Lightly moisten the top phyllo sheet with a few drops of water, and mark a criss-cross pattern with the point of a knife. Bake for 40 minutes. Serve hot.

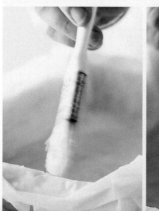

North African spiced Lamb

Serves 6
Preparation and
cooking time:
1³/₄ hours
Marinating time:
8–12 hours

1 teaspoon turmeric
1 teaspoon coarsely ground
pepper
¹/₂ teaspoon ground ginger
2 teaspoons ground
cinnamon
¹/₂ teaspoon cayenne
2³/₄ lb boneless lamb
shoulder, cubed
3 onions
4 garlic cloves
3 tablespoons sunflower oil
2 cinnamon sticks
2 cups prunes
4 tablespoons honey
1 small pumpkin, or piece of
pumpkin, about 2³/₄ lb
salt

• The day before serving, bring ²/₃ cup of water to a boil. Add the turmeric, coarsely ground pepper, ginger, 1 teaspoon of the cinnamon, and the cayenne. Remove from the heat, cover, and let cool. Then pour over the meat, cover, and marinate in the refrigerator for 8–12 hours.

• The following day, drain the lamb, reserving the marinade. Peel and slice the onions. Peel and chop the garlic. Cook the onions and garlic gently in 1 tablespoon of the oil until soft. Add the lamb, raise the heat, and stir for 1 minute. Add the marinade and enough water to cover. Salt generously and add the cinnamon sticks. Bring to a boil, then cover and simmer gently for 1 hour.

• When the lamb has cooked for 1 hour, add the prunes and 2 tablespoons honey. Cook for a further 30 minutes.

• Peel and seed the pumpkin and cut into chunks. Steam until tender, about 30 minutes. Purée in a food processor. Season to taste, then return to the pan and cook, stirring, until excess moisture evaporates. Stir in the remaining honey, oil, and cinnamon, and cook gently until thick.

• Remove the cinnamon sticks from the lamb stew, and serve with the pumpkin purée.

Serves 6
Preparation: 30 minutes
Cooking time: about 2 hours

2 carrots • 1 leek • 1 celery stalk • 1 bay leaf • 2 sprigs of fresh flat-leaf parsley
• 10 garlic cloves • 2 star anise • 1 large onion, studded with 2 whole cloves
• 3 lb boneless breast of veal, cut into pieces • 3 cups hard cider • 8 oz button
mushrooms • 3 tablespoons lemon juice • 24 boiling onions • 1$\frac{1}{2}$ tablespoons
unsalted butter • 1 teaspoon sugar • 1 cup crème fraîche • 2 pinches of grated
nutmeg • 1$\frac{1}{4}$ lb fresh tagliatelle • 2 egg yolks • salt and freshly ground pepper

Veal stew with cider and star anise

• Peel the carrots and cut into pieces. Clean the leek and slice the white part. Tie the green part together with the celery, bay leaf, and parsley. Put the unpeeled garlic cloves, star anise, clove-studded onion, carrots, leek slices, and herb bundle in a Dutch oven. Add the veal with the cider and enough water to cover. Bring to a boil, skimming off any foam, then season and cover. Simmer gently until the meat is tender, about 1$\frac{1}{2}$ hours.

• Clean the mushrooms, cut into quarters, and toss with most of the lemon juice. Add to the veal stew 15 minutes before the end of the cooking time.

• Peel the boiling onions and cook with the butter, sugar, and 1 cup of water for 20 minutes.

• Lift the veal and mushrooms out of the stew and keep warm in a serving dish along with the boiling onions. Strain the cooking liquid, reserving the garlic, then boil to reduce to about 2$\frac{1}{2}$ cups. Add the cooked garlic flesh, the crème fraîche, and nutmeg. Cook for 5 minutes, stirring occasionally.

• Cook the tagliatelle in boiling salted water according to package directions.

• Mix the egg yolks with the remaining lemon juice. Whisk in a spoonful of the crème fraîche sauce and blend well. Pour this mixture into the remaining sauce, whisking constantly, and cook over low heat for 2 minutes. Pour the sauce over the veal and vegetables, and serve with the well-drained tagliatelle.

Veal goulash with three peppers

• Peel and slice the onions. Core and seed all the bell peppers and cut into pieces. Peel the tomatoes and cut into pieces.

• Heat the oil in a pan over medium heat. Add the veal and bacon, and brown all over. Remove and set aside. Add the onions to the pan and cook until soft, then add the bell peppers. Stir for 1 minute, then stir in the tomatoes. Add the sugar and salt. Mix well, then lower the heat.

• Return the veal and bacon to the pan along with the paprika, and stir to mix. Cover and simmer until the veal is tender, $1\frac{1}{2}$–2 hours.

• Peel the potatoes and cook in boiling salted water, with the bay leaf, for 20 minutes or until tender. Drain well.

• Stir the crème fraîche into the goulash and heat gently for 1 minute, then serve with the boiled potatoes.

Serves 6
Preparation: 25 minutes
Cooking time: about
2 hours

3 large onions
2 red bell peppers
1 green bell pepper
2 yellow bell peppers
1 lb tomatoes
2 tablespoons oil
3 lb boneless veal shoulder, cubed
4 thick slices of bacon, cut into sticks
2 pinches of sugar
1 tablespoon paprika
6 medium-sized potatoes
1 bay leaf
2 tablespoons crème fraîche
salt

Marinated salmon with pink peppercorns

• Pat the salmon dry and place in a baking dish, skin-side down. Mix the sugar with 1¹/₂ tablespoons salt, the pink peppercorns, and 6 grinds of the peppermill. Sprinkle over the fish, then cover and marinate in the refrigerator for 8 hours.

• Preheat the oven to 425°F.

• Soften the onion in the butter over low heat without browning. Rinse the rice and add to the onion along with the bay leaf and thyme. Stir well. Bring 2¹/₂ cups of water to a boil, add the saffron, and pour over the rice. Cover and cook gently for 12 minutes or until tender.

• Wipe the shiitake mushrooms with a damp cloth, then cut into thick slices. Soften the shallots in the oil, then add the garlic and mushrooms. Mix well and cook over medium heat for 6–7 minutes. Season with salt.

• Drain the fish and rinse out the baking dish. Return the fish to the dish, skin-side up, and put into the oven to bake for 10 minutes.

• Stir the almonds into the rice, reserving a few for garnish.

• Remove the skin from the salmon, then serve accompanied by the mushrooms and rice, and garnished with the reserved almonds.

Serves 6
Preparation: 20 minutes
Cooking time: 20 minutes
Marinating time: 8 hours

6 pieces of salmon fillet, with skin, each about 6 oz
1¹/₂ tablespoons sugar
2 teaspoons pink peppercorns, crushed
1 onion, minced
1¹/₂ tablespoons unsalted butter
1¹/₂ cups basmati rice
¹/₂ bay leaf
1 sprig of fresh thyme
a few saffron threads
12 oz shiitake mushrooms
2 teaspoons chopped shallots
1 tablespoon olive oil
2 garlic cloves, crushed
2 tablespoons slivered almonds, lightly toasted
salt and freshly ground black pepper

Helpful hints for winter

• Pots of slowly simmering stews and soups are one of the best things about winter cooking.

• To ensure slow, even cooking, use pots and pans with a heavy base that will conduct the heat, and those that have a tight-fitting lid.

• It is worth investing in a spice ball or some cheesecloth for wrapping up herb sprigs and small whole spices. This makes it easier to remove them from stews and sauces at the end of cooking. It is important to take them out as there is nothing more unpleasant than biting into a whole peppercorn or clove that has been overlooked! If you don't make a cheesecloth-wrapped herb bundle (bouquet garni) or use a spice ball, be sure to remove the empty stems of herbs such as rosemary and thyme, bay leaves, and large whole spices such as cinnamon sticks.

• Many slow-simmered dishes benefit from being made in advance. Be sure to reheat gently for about 30 minutes before serving. The exception is dishes with egg- or cream-bound sauces, which should be made just before serving.

Shrimp stir-fry with Asian vegetables

• Remove the legs from the shrimp and cut the shell on the underside with scissors. Put the shrimp in a bowl and add 2 tablespoons sherry, 2 tablespoons oil, and 2 minced garlic cloves. Mix well, then cover and let marinate for 1 hour.

• Soak the mushrooms in hot water for 20 minutes. Drain. Cut off the stems, and chop the caps.

• Mix the cornstarch with the soy sauce and 2 tablespoons sherry.

Serves 4
Preparation and cooking time: 20 minutes
Marinating time: 1 hour

24 raw jumbo shrimp
5 tablespoons dry sherry
4 tablespoons sunflower oil
3 garlic cloves
3/4 oz dried Chinese mushrooms
2 teaspoons cornstarch
4 tablespoons soy sauce
2 shallots, minced
1 red bell pepper, thinly sliced
1 cup snow peas
12 oz frozen stir-fry vegetables
1 teaspoon sugar
2 tablespoons chopped fresh cilantro or parsley
2 tablespoons unsalted butter

• Heat the remaining oil in a wok. Add the shallots, remaining garlic clove, crushed, the bell pepper, and snow peas, and stir-fry for 2 minutes. Add the mushrooms and stir-fry for 1 minute, then add the frozen vegetables and stir-fry for another minute. Add the sugar and the cornstarch mixture. Bring to a boil and cook, stirring frequently, for 2 minutes.

• Drain the shrimp, reserving the liquid. In a frying pan, cook the shrimp until they turn pink, 2–3 minutes per side.

• Put the vegetables in a serving dish and sprinkle with the cilantro. Surround with the shrimp. Pour the shrimp marinating liquid and remaining sherry into the frying pan and bring to a boil. Add the butter and cook, stirring, until melted. Pour over the shrimp and serve.

Coconut-curry risotto with cashews

- Rinse the rice. Heat the vegetable stock and season with salt if necessary.
- Heat 2 tablespoons of the oil in a sauté pan, add the onion and rice, and cook, stirring constantly, until the rice is translucent. Add the curry powder and stir for a few seconds. Stir in the carrots, then add the vegetable stock. Simmer over low heat, uncovered, until all the liquid is absorbed, about 20 minutes.
- Clean and slice the mushrooms. Heat the remaining oil in a frying pan, add the mushrooms and garlic, and cook until all the liquid that comes from the mushrooms has evaporated. Season with salt and pepper.
- Peel the tomatoes and cut into small dice. Sprinkle with salt and let drain in a strainer. Drain the corn. Toast the cashews in a dry pan.
- When the rice is cooked, stir in the coconut milk, mushrooms, tomatoes, corn, and cashews. Heat through gently, about 1 minute.
- Sprinkle with the parsley before serving.

Serves 4
Preparation and cooking
time: 30 minutes

1³/₄ cups risotto rice
4 cups vegetable stock
3 tablespoons sunflower oil
1 onion, minced
1 tablespoon curry powder
2 carrots, peeled and diced
8 oz button mushrooms
1 garlic clove, chopped
2 large tomatoes
1 small can corn kernels
¹/₂ cup unsalted cashews
1 cup coconut milk
1 tablespoon chopped fresh
flat-leaf parsley
salt and freshly ground pepper

Serves 6
Preparation: 30 minutes
Cooking time: 2 hours

1 boned shoulder of lamb (not rolled) • 7 oz cooked ham • $\frac{1}{3}$ cup raisins • 3 slices of white bread • 3 tablespoons milk • 12 large garlic cloves• 2 shallots, minced • 3$\frac{1}{2}$ tablespoons olive oil • $\frac{1}{3}$ cup pine nuts • 1 tablespoon chopped fresh chives • 1 teaspoon fresh thyme leaves • grated zest of 1 lemon • 2 eggs • 1 teaspoon ground cumin • 1 tablespoon ras-el-hanout spice mixture (see box page 10) • 1$\frac{1}{4}$ cups dry white wine • 6 carrots, cut into thick rounds • 2 cups quick-cook couscous • salt and freshly ground pepper

Stuffed shoulder of lamb on a bed of couscous

• Trim the lamb shoulder to obtain an even-shaped piece. Chop the lamb trimmings along with the ham.

• Soak the raisins in hot water; soak the bread in the milk. Peel and chop 2 of the garlic cloves. Cook them with the shallots in $\frac{1}{2}$ tablespoon of the oil until soft.

• Mix together the chopped meat, drained raisins, cooked garlic mixture, pine nuts, chives, thyme, lemon zest, beaten eggs, cumin, and pepper. Squeeze the bread dry and add to the meat mixture. Spread this stuffing over the lamb shoulder, then roll up and tie to secure.

• Brown the lamb in 2 tablespoons of the oil. Lower the heat, and add the remaining unpeeled garlic cloves, the ras-el-hanout, white wine, and salt. Cover and cook over low heat for 1$\frac{1}{2}$ hours, turning the meat occasionally. Add the carrots and cook for a further 30 minutes.

• Cook the couscous in salted water, with the remaining oil, according to package directions. Fluff with a fork and keep hot.

• Skim the fat from the lamb cooking broth. Scoop out the garlic cloves and squeeze the pulp back into the broth. Pile the couscous in the middle of a platter and surround with the sliced lamb and carrots. Serve the garlicky broth as a sauce.

Chicken in sherry cream sauce

Serves 4
Preparation: 25 minutes
Cooking time: 45 minutes

6 chicken thighs • 1 tablespoon sunflower oil • 3 shallots, thinly sliced • 3 carrots, diced • 1 sprig of fresh thyme • 1 bay leaf • 2 cinnamon sticks • 1 chicken bouillon cube • 1 garlic clove, crushed • $^1\!/_2$ cup + 2 tablespoons sherry • 16–20 fresh lychees • $1^1\!/_3$ cups bulgur wheat or cracked wheat • 2 tablespoons crème fraîche • 2 egg yolks • salt

• Season the chicken pieces with salt. Heat the oil in a pan, add the chicken pieces, and brown on all sides. Add the shallots and cook for 1 minute. Stir in the carrots, thyme, bay leaf, and cinnamon sticks. Crumble in the bouillon cube and add the garlic. Lower the heat, add $^1\!/_2$ cup of the sherry, and cover immediately. Simmer gently for 30 minutes.

• Peel the lychees. Cook the bulgur or cracked wheat in boiling salted water according to package directions.

• Add the crème fraîche to the chicken and cook for a further 10 minutes. Whisk together the egg yolks and the remaining 2 tablespoons sherry. Remove the chicken from the heat and stir in the egg mixture, mixing well. Taste for seasoning, then stir in the lychees. Reheat for 30 seconds, stirring constantly; do not allow to boil. Serve with the bulgur or cracked wheat.

Serves 6
Preparation: 30 minutes
Cooking time: 3 hours 20 minutes

2 tablespoons olive oil • 3-lb beef chuck roast, neatly tied •
1¹/₂ lb onions, sliced • 2 tablespoons sugar • 2 cups sliced
carrots • 1 cup peeled and diced celeriac • 1 head of garlic
• 2 cups tomato purée • 3 tablespoons wine vinegar
• 2 teaspoons ground allspice • ¹/₂ teaspoon ground
cinnamon • 2 bay leaves • 2 sprigs of fresh thyme
• 1 teaspoon coarsely ground black pepper • ²/₃ cup raisins
• ¹/₂ cup Madeira • salt • **For the vegetable purée:** 1¹/₂ lb
potatoes • ¹/₂ celeriac, peeled • 2 tablespoons crème fraîche

Sweet-sour
braised beef

• Heat the oil in a Dutch oven and add the beef. Brown all over, then remove. Add the onions to the pot and cook until soft. Add the sugar, carrots, diced celeriac, 1 chopped garlic clove, the tomato purée, and vinegar. Stir well.

• Rub the beef with the allspice and cinnamon, then return to the pot. Add the bay leaves, thyme, coarse pepper, salt, and remaining unpeeled garlic cloves. Cover tightly and cook over low heat for about 3 hours or until the meat is tender, adding water if necessary during cooking.

• Soak the raisins in the Madeira, and add to the beef 30 minutes before the end of the cooking time.

• To make the vegetable purée, peel and chop the potatoes. Place in a pan of cold water, add salt, and bring to a boil. Add the chopped celeriac. Cook for 20 minutes or until tender. Drain well, then purée by beating with a hand-held electric mixer. Beat in the crème fraîche.

• Slice the beef and pour the cooking liquid over. Serve with the vegetable purée.

West Indian pork curry with sweet potatoes

• Peel and mince the onions. Heat 1 tablespoon oil in a frying pan, add the onions, and cook until soft. Peel and crush the garlic. Peel and grate the ginger.

• Heat the remaining oil in a Dutch oven over medium heat. Add the pork and brown on all sides. Stir in the honey, then add the soy sauce and colombo. Stir in the cooked onions, the garlic, ginger, and tomato paste. Then stir in 1 cup of water and bring slowly to a boil. Season lightly with salt and pepper, and simmer gently for $1\frac{1}{4}$ hours.

• Peel the sweet potatoes and cut into pieces. Cook in boiling salted water until tender, about 20 minutes. Drain, then purée. Stir in the butter, grated nutmeg, salt, and pepper. Serve hot, with the curry.

Serves 6
Preparation: 25 minutes
Cooking time: $1\frac{1}{2}$ hours

8 oz onions
3 tablespoons sunflower oil
8 garlic cloves
1 piece of fresh ginger, about 1 inch long
$2\frac{3}{4}$ lb boneless pork shoulder, cut in $1\frac{1}{2}$-inch cubes
3 tablespoons honey
3 tablespoons soy sauce
2 tablespoons colombo (West Indian curry spice – see box opposite)
1 tablespoon tomato paste
$2\frac{3}{4}$ lb sweet potatoes
2 tablespoons unsalted butter
grated nutmeg, salt, and freshly ground pepper

Colombo (West Indian curry spice)

3 garlic cloves • 2 fresh, hot, red chili peppers • 1 teaspoon ground coriander • 1 teaspoon mustard powder • pinch of turmeric

• Peel and crush the garlic. Remove seeds from the chilies and mince. Combine all ingredients and mix to a paste.

• The mixture will keep in a refrigerator for up to 6 weeks.

Lamb curry with pistachios

• Heat the oil in a Dutch oven, add the cubes of lamb, and brown on all sides. Stir in the onions, garlic, and bell pepper, then lower the heat and cook for 10 minutes. Stir in the curry powder and cook for 2 more minutes. Pour in just enough water to cover the lamb. Stir in the tomato paste and bring to a boil. Season with salt, then cover and simmer gently for $1\frac{1}{4}$ hours. Add the apple and coconut milk, and cook for a further 30 minutes.

• Rinse the rice and cook in boiling salted water for 10–12 minutes or until tender.

• Peel the mangoes. Cut the flesh from the central seed and cut into cubes.

• Drain the rice and stir in the pistachios. Transfer the curry to a warmed platter and serve, with the mango and rice alongside.

Serves 6
Preparation: 25 minutes
Cooking time: 2 hours

2 tablespoons sunflower oil
3 lb boneless lamb shoulder, cubed
3 large onions, minced
3 garlic cloves, chopped
1 red bell pepper, finely diced
2 tablespoons curry powder
$\frac{1}{4}$ cup tomato paste
1 apple, peeled and cubed
$1\frac{1}{4}$ cups coconut milk
2 cups basmati rice
2 mangoes
$\frac{1}{2}$ cup unsalted pistachios
salt

Chicken fricassée with lime and coconut milk

• Finely grate the zest from the lime.

• Heat the oil in a sauté pan, add the chicken and shallots, and cook until browned. Add the salt, ground cinnamon, garlic, sugar, and cayenne. Mix the tomato paste with 3 tablespoons of water and add to the pan, mixing well. Add the coconut milk and bring to a boil, then add the cinnamon stick and lime zest. Cook over low heat for 30 minutes.

• Cook the rice in boiling salted water according to package directions.

• Peel the kiwi fruit and cut into cubes. Drain the rice and stir in the kiwi fruit.

• Just before serving, squeeze the lime and stir 2–3 tablespoons juice into the chicken fricassée. Serve hot, with the rice.

Serves 4
Preparation: 20 minutes
Cooking time: 40 minutes

1 lime
1 tablespoon sunflower oil
6 chicken thighs
2 shallots, chopped
$\frac{1}{2}$ teaspoon ground cinnamon
2 garlic cloves, chopped
2 pinches of sugar
2–3 pinches of cayenne
1 tablespoon tomato paste
1 cup coconut milk
1 cinnamon stick
1$\frac{1}{2}$ cups red rice
2 kiwi fruit
salt

Fish couscous with sofrito sauce

Serves 6
Preparation time:
40 minutes
Cooking time: 40 minutes

2 cups couscous
2 slices of white bread
4 tablespoons milk
1-lb piece of pumpkin
4 carrots
2 zucchini
1 red bell pepper
1 large onion
1 head of garlic, unpeeled, cut horizontally in half
1 striped or silver mullet, about 2³/₄ lb, scaled and cut into pieces, head reserved
2 tablespoons ras-el-hanout spice mixture (see box page 10)
1 celery stalk
1 tablespoon tomato paste
4 tablespoons olive oil
10 oz haddock fillet, cut into small pieces
1 tablespoon chopped fresh parsley
1 egg
6 hake or whiting steaks
4 tablespoons unsalted butter
flour
salt and freshly ground pepper

• **For the sofrito sauce:**
3 garlic cloves, chopped
2 onions, minced
2 tablespoons olive oil
6 tablespoons ground almonds
4 tablespoons fresh bread crumbs
4 tomatoes, peeled and diced
cayenne

• Mix the couscous with 2 cups salted water and let absorb. Moisten the bread with the milk. Peel and coarsely chop the pumpkin and carrots. Chop the zucchini and bell pepper. Peel the onion and tie up in a square of cheesecloth with the garlic and the fish head.

• Bring 6 cups water to a boil in the bottom of a couscous steamer (or use an ordinary steamer lined with cheesecloth). Add the ras-el-hanout, all the vegetables, the tomato paste, and 1 tablespoon of the oil. Mix well. Add the cheesecloth bundle. Put the couscous in the top section and place over the water. Cover and steam for 30 minutes.

• Squeeze the bread dry. Combine with the haddock pieces, parsley, egg, salt, and pepper. Refrigerate for 15 minutes. Season the hake with salt.

• Tip the couscous into a bowl and add the butter, in pieces. Cover and keep warm. Remove the cheesecloth bundle from the vegetable broth. Add the mullet pieces to the broth and simmer gently for 3 minutes. Add the hake and cook for a further 7–8 minutes.

• Shape the haddock mixture into small dumplings. Coat in flour and fry in the remaining 3 tablespoons oil.

• For the sauce, soften the garlic and onions in the oil. Add the almonds and bread crumbs, and cook gently for 2 minutes, stirring. Raise the heat, add the tomatoes, and cook until thickened. Season with salt, pepper, and cayenne.

• To serve, pile the couscous in the middle of a dish and surround with the vegetables, fish pieces, and dumplings. Serve with the cooking broth and sofrito sauce.

Serves 4
Preparation: 40 minutes
Cooking time: 1 hour

10 oz carrots • 1 garlic clove, peeled • 1 bay leaf • $^1/_2$ vegetable bouillon cube • $^2/_3$ cup basmati rice • 1 lb frozen leaf spinach • 2 eggs • $^1/_3$ cup grated Parmesan • 4 tablespoons unsalted butter • $^1/_4$ cup flour • 2 tablespoons lowfat milk • 2 pinches of grated nutmeg • 3 pinches of ground cinnamon • 1 package cream of asparagus soup mix • $^1/_2$ cup crème fraîche • 1 tablespoon lemon juice • 1 teaspoon chopped fresh tarragon • salt • For the canapés: 1 apple • 1 tablespoon lemon juice • 4 small goat cheeses

Rice and vegetable terrine with goat-cheese canapés

• Peel the carrots and cut lengthwise into quarters. Bring 2 cups water to a boil. Add the carrots, garlic, bay leaf, and bouillon cube. Cover and cook for 20 minutes. Cook the rice in boiling salted water according to package directions. Cook the spinach in boiling salted water, then drain well. When cool, squeeze dry and chop.

• Preheat the oven to 400°F. Drain the carrots, reserving the cooking liquid. Chop and add to the drained rice along with the beaten eggs and Parmesan. Melt the butter in a saucepan and stir in the flour. Whisk in the carrot broth and bring to a boil. Remove from the heat and add the milk, nutmeg, cinnamon, and spinach. Stir well.

• Butter a 9-inch-long terrine mold or loaf pan. Pour in half the rice and press down well. Top with half the spinach mixture. Cover with the remaining rice and finish with the rest of the spinach. Dot with the butter and bake for 30 minutes.

• For the canapés, peel and core the apple. Cut 4 rounds, each about $^1/_2$ inch thick, from the apple and rub with lemon juice. Place on a greased baking sheet and top each slice with a goat cheese. Bake for 10 minutes (put in the oven 20 minutes after the rice terrine).

• Bring 2 cups water to a boil and stir in the asparagus soup mix. Simmer for 5 minutes, stirring constantly. Add the crème fraîche, lemon juice, and tarragon.

• Carefully unmold the terrine and serve, with the goat-cheese canapés and asparagus sauce.

Grilled vegetable and lamb lasagne

• Peel and mince the onions and garlic. Heat 1 tablespoon of the oil in a frying pan, add the onion and lamb, and cook until browned, crushing the meat with a fork to crumble. Add the tomato purée, garlic, thyme, bay leaf, cinnamon, 2 pinches of sugar, the nutmeg, and $1/2$ cup water. Season with salt and pepper. Stir well, then cover and simmer over medium heat until the sauce thickens, about 15 minutes.

• Cut the eggplants and zucchini lengthwise into slices about $1/2$ inch thick, and brush with oil. Grill on a hot ridged grill pan (or under a preheated broiler), along with the bell peppers, for about 6 minutes on one side, 4 on the other. Peel the peppers and purée with a pinch of sugar and salt to taste. Season the eggplant and zucchini slices, and spread with a thin layer of garlic purée.

• Preheat the oven to 425°F.

• Oil a baking dish. Put in a layer of eggplant, then a layer of lamb sauce, and then a layer of zucchini. Continue layering, finishing with a mixed layer of eggplant and zucchini. Sprinkle with the chopped basil, Parmesan shavings, and bell pepper purée. Drizzle with the remaining olive oil and sprinkle with the shredded cheese. Bake for 30 minutes. Serve hot, in the baking dish.

Serves 4
Preparation: 25 minutes
Cooking time: 50 minutes

3 onions
2 garlic cloves
3 tablespoons olive oil
1 lb ground lamb
2 cups tomato purée
$1/2$ teaspoon fresh thyme leaves
1 bay leaf
$1/2$ teaspoon ground cinnamon
sugar
pinch of grated nutmeg
2 eggplants
3 zucchini
2 red bell peppers
small jar of garlic purée
12 large, fresh basil leaves
$1/2$ cup Parmesan shavings
$1/2$ cup shredded cheese, preferably Gruyère
salt and freshly ground pepper

North African spiced veal shanks with honey

• Combine the ras-el-hanout, turmeric, pepper, ginger, and 1 teaspoon salt.

• Heat the oil in a Dutch oven, add the slices of veal, and brown on both sides over medium heat. Remove the meat and add the onions, cooking until soft. Coat the veal slices in the spice mixture and return to the pan, placing them on top of the onions. Add the wine and $\frac{1}{2}$ cup water. Bring to a boil. Season with salt, cover, and simmer for 1 hour. Add the honey and cinnamon sticks. Cook, covered, for a further 30 minutes.

• Meanwhile, put the apricots, sugar, and vanilla bean in a pan with just enough water to cover. Cook until the water has almost all evaporated. Discard the vanilla bean. Remove from the heat.

• In another pan, cook the couscous in boiling salted water, with the butter, according to package directions. Serve the veal shanks with the couscous and apricots, and the cooking broth on the side.

Serves 4
Preparation: 35 minutes
Cooking time 1 hour
50 minutes

1 heaped tablespoon
ras-el-hanout spice mixture
(see box page 10)
1 teaspoon turmeric
1 teaspoon pepper
$\frac{1}{4}$ teaspoon ground ginger
2 tablespoons sunflower oil
4 meaty slices of veal shank
3 onions, chopped
$\frac{1}{2}$ cup white wine
2 tablespoons honey
2 cinnamon sticks
2 cups dried apricots
2 tablespoons sugar
1 vanilla bean
$1\frac{1}{2}$ cups couscous
3 tablespoons unsalted butter
salt

Tea-smoked duck breasts

• Score the skin of the duck breasts in a criss-cross pattern. Season with salt and pepper. Trim the mushroom stems, then clean the caps.

• Preheat the broiler. Combine the orange zest, tea, sugar, and cinnamon. Line the bottom of a heavy sauté pan with foil and spread the tea mixture on top. Stir over high heat until the mixture starts to smoke. Lay a rack over the pan and put the duck breasts on the rack, skin-side up. Cook in the tea smoke over high heat for 5 minutes. Lift up the rack with the duck breasts and set it in a broiler pan. Cook under the broiler for 10 minutes. Turn the breasts and cook for 8 more minutes.

• Heat the oil in a frying pan, add the shallots and garlic, and cook for 1 minute. Add the mushrooms and cook for 10 minutes over high heat. Season with salt.

• Meanwhile, pour off some of the duck fat and sauté the sliced potatoes in it.

• Keep the duck breasts warm. Discard the excess fat from the broiler pan, then pour in the sherry and stir to mix with the cooking juices. Pour this sauce over the mushrooms. Slice the duck breasts thinly across the grain and arrange on plates with the mushrooms and the sautéed potatoes. Serve immediately.

Serves 4
Preparation and cooking time: 35 minutes

2 boneless duck breast halves, each about 14 oz
1 lb black trumpet mushrooms
pared zest of 1 orange, in fine strips
$1/3$ cup Lapsang Souchong tea leaves
2 tablespoons brown sugar
2 teaspoons ground cinnamon
1 tablespoon sunflower oil
3 shallots, minced
2 garlic cloves, minced
1 lb small potatoes, parboiled and sliced
2 tablespoons sherry
salt and freshly ground pepper

index of recipes

Poached chicken breasts with tuna sauce 32

Rice and vegetable terrine with goat-cheese canapés 86

Rice salad with poached eggs 12

Seafood kebabs with mango sauce 36

Shrimp stir-fry with Asian vegetables 70

Spanakopita 58

Spanish-style sole fillets 39

Spanish-style stuffed veal 31

Spiced pork with rice and figs 33

Stuffed shoulder of lamb on a bed of couscous 75

Sweet-sour braised beef 77

Tea-smoked duck breasts 92

Veal goulash with three peppers 64

Veal stew with cider and star anise 62

Veal stuffed with spinach and ham 34

Vegetable couscous with quail-egg kebabs 56

Vegetable kebabs with red sauce 14

Vegetable tourte 44

West Indian pork curry with sweet potatoes 78